THE TOLKIEN
FAMILY ALBUM

TOLKIEN

THE
CENTENARY
1892-1992

TOLKIEN

THE TOLKIEN
FAMILY ALBUM

John & Priscilla Tolkien

Boston
Houghton Mifflin Company
1992

For information about permission to reproduce
selections from this book, write to
Permissions, Houghton Mifflin Company,
2 Park Street, Boston, Massachusetts 02108

CIP data is available.

ISBN 0–395–59938–5

1 3 5 7 9 10 8 6 4 2

PICTURE CREDITS
& ACKNOWLEDGEMENTS

Space does not permit us to thank individually all the people who have helped us in the course of preparing this book but we do wish to make acknowledgement to the following for giving us permission to use the material to illustrate the text:

South Africa Library, Cape Town, for the print of Cape Town Cathedral and Main Street (page 15); The National Maritime Museum for the print of S.S. Guelph (page 18); Birmingham Public Libraries for prints of Sarehole Mill, 2 Gracewell Road, Sam Gamgee, The Birmingham Oratory, King Edward's School, the Suffields and The Barrows Stores (pages 20, 22, 23, 25, 14, 26); Evesham Library for the print of Dresden House, 1904 (page 27); Stephen Gateley for the photograph of his great-grandfather and for the correspondence between Uncle Jessop and his great-grandfather (pages 28, 34); Mrs Dennis Paxman for the photograph of the Swiss trip (page 31); The Bodleian Library for the cover of the Exeter College magazine, for J.R.R.T.'s trench-map and written orders (pages 32,40); Canon Stewart for the print of the interior of St Mary's Church, Warwick (page 38); the Imperial War Museum for the print of Ypres (page 39); Oxford University Press for entries for 'hobbit' and 'walrus' in the Oxford English Dictionary (pages 88, 42); University of Leeds Archives for prints of Leeds University, the record of J.R.R.T.'s salary and the extract from *The Gryphon* (pages 43, 46, 49); Robert Burchfield for his article in *The Independent* of 4 March 1989, from which we quote (page 53); Walter Hooper for his photograph of C. S. Lewis (page 66); Professor Meredith Thompson for his photographs (pages 68, 72); Elaine Griffiths for her photograph (page 69); the Warden and Fellows of Merton College, Oxford, for the print of Professor Garrod (page 76); Westgate Library, Oxford, for the print of Eights Week (page 77); Joy Hill for access to J.R.R.T.'s fan mail, from which a fan letter is reproduced (page 84); Charles Noad for his photographs of Vera Chapman and of the Tolkien Society at J.R.R.T.'s graveside in Wolvercote Cemetery, Oxford (pages 85, 88); *The Daily Telegraph* for their obituary of J.R.R.T. on 3 September 1973 (page 88); Richard Spilsbury for his photographs of Edith's piano, the house in Warwick, Merton College, the Rocket Award and 21 Merton Street, Oxford (pages 30, 37, 52, 79, 87).

Finally, we should like to express our warm appreciation of our friends and colleagues, Richard Spilsbury and Louise Stewart, who undertook all the picture research and contributed so much to our enjoyment by their unfailing interest and enthusiasm.

PREFACE

As a family we hoard relics from the past. After the deaths of our parents Priscilla, by general agreement, kept in her home the considerable collection of family photographs. When John moved back to the Oxford area in 1987 he and Priscilla began to work together on identifying and cataloguing these before too much was forgotten. We began to realise how much was revealed of the whole period of our parents' lives, from the turn of the century to the present time.

By this time the centenary of our father's birth was approaching, an occasion for both personal and public celebration, and so out of our private collection we began to make this book: an album of memories of the eldest and youngest of J.R.R. Tolkien's four children. Our aim is to give an affectionate picture of J.R.R. Tolkien's life and work, illustrated by glimpses of where he lived in a century of change between the end of the Victorian Age and our own day.

John Benjamin Tolkien *m.* Mary Jane Stow
1807-1896
(piano manufacturer and
music-seller in Birmingham)

Arthur Reuel *m.* Mabel   Florence *m.* Tom   Grace *m.* William   Mabel *m.* Tom   4 sons
Tolkien   Suffield   Hadley   Mountain   Mitton
1857–1896   1870–1904
(bank manager)

John Ronald Reuel Tolkien   *m.*   Edith Bratt   Hilary Arthur Reuel Tolkien
1892–1973   1889–1971   1894–1976

John   Michael *m.* Joan Griffiths   Faith (1)   *m.*   Christopher   *m.*   (2) Baillie   Priscilla
b. 1917   1920–1984   1916–1982   Faulconbridge   *b.* 1924   Knapheis   *b.* 1929
                         b. 1928

Irene (1) *m.* Michael *m.* (2) Jan   Joan *m.* Hugh   Judith *m.*   Alan   Simon *m.* Tracy
Ferrier   *b.* 1943   Turner   *b.* 1945   Baker   *b.* 1951   Crombleholme   *b.* 1959   Sternber

Catherine   Ruth   Mandy   Royd   Michael   Freya   Piers   Nicholas
b. 1969   *b.* 1982   *b.* 1967   *b.* 1969   *b.* 1975   *b.* 1976   *b.* 1979   *b.* 1990

FAMILY TREE

John Suffield *m.* Emily Sparrow
1802–1891
(Birmingham
draper)

2 sons	May *m.* Walter		Mabel *m.* Arthur		Jane *m.* Edwin		William *m.* Beatrice		
	1865–1936 Incledon		1870–1904 Tolkien		1872–1963 Neave		1874–1904 Bartlett		
	(business man)								

== *m.* Magdalen Matthews   Marjorie   Mary
                                 1891–1973   1895–1940

Gabriel *m.* (1) June (2) Kay   Julian *m.* Glynis   Paul *m.* Ann
b. 1931   *b.* 1935   *b.* 1938

Adam   Rachel   Angela   Christopher *m.* Angela   Timothy *m.* Sue   Nicholas   Stephen   Dominic   Zoe
b. 1969   *b.* 1971

2 sons

THE TOLKIEN
FAMILY ALBUM

John Ronald Reuel Tolkien was a man who came to be deeply identified with the England of his childhood - that area of the West Midlands which he was to make famous in his stories of the Shire, homeland of the Hobbits. But, in fact, his origins lay in a distant country: he was born on 3 January 1892, in Bloemfontein, South Africa, the first son of Arthur Tolkien and his wife Mabel, née Suffield.

Both families came from the Midlands, near or in Birmingham: Arthur had left his native England to take up a job for the Bank of South Africa (where prospects for advancement were far greater than with Lloyds, in Birmingham) and soon he became manager of the Bank of Africa in Bloemfontein in the Orange Free State.

Grandfather and Grandmother Suffield

Arthur Tolkien (seated, left) and his bank staff

Cape Town Cathedral, c. 1890

Mabel followed him to South Africa a year later and in 1891 they were married in Cape Town Cathedral. The family lived in Bloemfontein, over the bank in Maitland Street: beyond were the dusty, treeless plains of the veldt.

From the few of Mabel's letters that survive, we know that our grandmother heartily disliked the inhospitable climate: and we can also see her elegant and decorative handwriting, which almost certainly influenced Ronald's interest in design and calligraphy later in his life.

She also disliked the Boer attitude to the native servants: a family photograph taken in 1892 included the nurse, the maid and the house-boy Isaak.

In February 1894 Mabel gave birth to her second son, Hilary. It was a particularly hot year, which had adverse effects on Ronald's health and it was with some relief that Mabel prepared to take her two sons back to England for a short holiday in April 1895.

Years later, Ronald described to us the powerful sense he had during the preparations for that voyage of the weight of emotion between his parents at their coming separation. He retained an image of extraordinary clarity of his father painting 'A.R. Tolkien' on their cabin trunk, an item that Ronald kept and treasured in memory of his father. Of the long voyage home on the SS Guelph he remembered two brilliantly sharp images: the first of looking down from the deck of the ship into the clear waters of the Indian Ocean far below, which was full of lithe brown and black bodies diving for coins thrown by the passengers; the second was of pulling into a harbour at sunrise and seeing a great city set on the hillside above, which he realised much later in life must have been Lisbon.

SS Guelph

Ronald spent only three of his eighty-one years in South Africa, but it made a deep and lasting impression on him, and he always regretted never returning to the country of his birth. He is still remembered in his birthplace: in 1984 a memorial service was held in Bloemfontein Cathedral, where Ronald was christened in 1892; and a plaque was unveiled in Maitland Street on the site of the Bank.

Mabel took the boys to stay with her family in King's Heath, Birmingham: then, in February 1896 she received a telegram announcing Arthur's sudden illness. The next day he died carried off swiftly by rheumatic fever. Ronald always grieved that he knew his father for such a short time.

Death of Mr. Tolkien.

It is our sad duty to announce the death of Mr. A. R. Tolkien, the able and respected manager of the Bloemfontein branch of the Bank of Africa. About four months ago Mr. Tolkien was seized with an attack of rheumatic fever, from which he never fully recovered. About three weeks ago he went to the Conquered Territory to recruit, and, although on his return he was still weak, yet he appeared to be in good spirits until Friday evening, when he fell ill again. The patient did not at first surmise how bad his case was, and as late as Friday afternoon he expressed the hope that he would be able to resume his duties on Wednesday next, so as to enable his accountant to attend the cricket match on that day. But during the night hæmorrhage set in, and on Saturday afternoon, after having received the sacrament, Mr. Tolkien breathed his last, in the presence of the Dean, the nurse Sister Flora, and Mr. van Zyl, the accountant.

Mr. Tolkien was a native of Birmingham, and had only reached the age of forty. He was for years a trusted official in Lloyd's Bank in his native town, and joined the Bank of Africa about nine years ago. The last six years were spent in Bloemfontein, where the deceased, through his sterling qualities, gained the esteem of all with whom he came in contact.

Mrs. Tolkien, who is at present in England with her two children, was to have sailed for South Africa on the 2nd March. She was cabled to on Saturday morning to expect the worst, and will have the sincere sympathy of a large circle of friends.

The funeral took place yesterday afternoon and was largely attended. There was a full choral service in the Cathedral.

In the summer of 1896 Mabel found a cottage in the lovely countryside near Moseley, just south of Birmingham. Nearby was Sarehole Mill, which fascinated the boys, though they were terrified of the miller's son, whom Ronald named 'The White Ogre'. The area at that time was almost entirely rural. Ronald retained strong memories of the four years spent there and of flowers – such as wild daffodils – in the fields. It was, therefore, with great sadness that, driving to Birmingham in the mid-1930s he saw the whole region being built over and his beloved fields disappearing.

ABOVE: *Gracewell Road*

LEFT: *Sarehole Mill*

In those days little boys did not have their hair cut for some years after babyhood, and Mabel left it longer than most, so Ronald and Hilary were looked upon with great suspicion by the local children, who called them 'wenches'! That the children should use this archaic term interested J.R.R.T. greatly in later years.

The boys picked up other archaic and dialect words: one of these was 'gamgee' for cotton wool: a local man named Samson Gamgee had become a household name for the surgical dressing he had invented. The name lodged itself in Ronald's memory, later to emerge as Sam Gamgee, Frodo's faithful companion in *The Lord of the Rings*.

In 1900 Mabel became a Catholic, much to the disapproval of her family, the Suffields, and her husband's family, who promptly withdrew all financial support. Their hostility affected her health, but not her faith, and she began to instruct her sons in the Catholic religion. She also taught her sons the elements of Latin, French, English and drawing, and it was now that Ronald started to learn calligraphy. A delightful 'coded' letter made when Ronald was seven has survived from this period.

Sam Gamgee

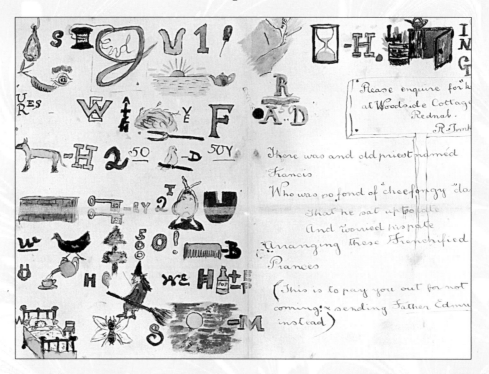

It was also in 1900 that Ronald started school: at King Edward's Grammar School on New Street in Birmingham. The journey from Sarehole was too long for a little boy on his own so eventually the family found a house near the Oratory on the Hagley Road, a very different environment from rural Sarehole, and Ronald resented this. Two years later, the boys were enrolled at St Phillip's Grammar School, a Catholic school run by the Oratory Fathers.

LEFT: *Ronald, aged nine*

BELOW: *Birmingham Oratory*

Among the Fathers was Father Francis Morgan, who was of Anglo-Spanish descent, his family being in the wine trade, and the Spanish connection contributed to the young Ronald's developing interest in languages.

Father Francis Morgan

St Phillip's proved to be a poor contrast to King Edward's and in 1903 Ronald won a scholarship and returned to his old school. The next year Mabel was taken ill with diabetes. Father Francis arranged that the family should rent rooms in the lodge cottage at Rednal, where the Oratory Fathers still have a country retreat. There, in November 1904, she died, at the early age of thirty-four. She was buried in the churchyard at St Peter's RC Church at Bromsgrove.

Father Francis became guardian to the two young orphans, and after an unhappy period with their aunt, Beatrice Suffield, who showed them no affection, he found lodgings for them in Duchess Road, some small distance from the Oratory and King Edward's.

King Edward's School

Ronald enjoyed his schooldays at King Edward's. He was good at games, especially rugby, being made captain of the rugby team from 1910 to 1911. He was also active in the Debating Society. The backbone of the curriculum was Classics. J.R.R.T. was able to speak both Latin and Greek, and his great interest in languages was encouraged. He even started to invent his own, 'private' languages at this time.

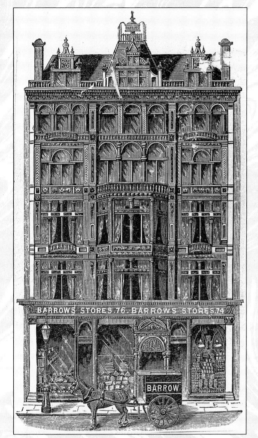

ABOVE: *King Edward's School first XI (J.R.R.T. fourth from right in back row)*

LEFT: *Barrows Stores*

Ronald and three of his friends - Christopher Wiseman, Robert Gilson and Geoffrey Smith - formed a 'Tea Club', the TCBS, meeting regularly at Barrows Stores in Corporation Street for discussions and recitations. The boarding house in Duchess Road was run by a Mrs Faulkner, an active member of the Oratory parish. Staying there at the same time was a girl called Edith Bratt.

A small, compact oak desk, and in front of it a woman sitting in a pretty Edwardian harp-shaped chair writing letters: this is the most powerful continuing image we retain of our mother throughout her long life; of her early life, of course, our memories are fragmentary, although a great deal was told to us from those early days.

Our mother, Edith, was born in Gloucester in 1889, though she spent most of her early life in the Handsworth area of Birmingham with her mother, Frances, and cousin, Jenny Grove. Frances Bratt died when Edith was 14, and she was sent away to Dresden House School, a boarding-school in Evesham run by two sisters, the Misses Watts, who had received their musical education in Dresden. These ladies placed a particular emphasis on music, and it was at the school that Edith first developed her great love, and talent, for playing the piano.

Despite a strict regime - which included rising at 6 a.m. to practise for two hours before breakfast in an unheated room even on the coldest days - there were high-spirited games and midnight feasts. Our mother would recount with pleasure how the neighbours spied on them from behind lace curtains and eventually reported their activities to the authorities. The school bell was rung and then they knew they were in trouble!

Dresden House School

After school, Edith's legal guardian, Stephen Gateley, the family solicitor, found her rooms with Mrs Faulkner in a genteel boarding-house in Duchess Road, Edgbaston. Mrs Faulkner gave musical soirées, at which Edith would play, but would never allow Edith to practise! Edith's life there seems to have been rather restricted. She once described going to a matinée at the Theatre Royal in Birmingham (she had a lifelong enjoyment of the theatre) and being told she must take a book to read in the interval to avoid the risk of being talked to by strangers!

Stephen Gateley

Edith, aged nineteen

Edith was nineteen when Ronald and Hilary Tolkien came to live at the boarding-house. Within a short time, Edith and Ronald, drawn together by their similar age and circumstances, had become fast friends and allies against 'The Old Lady' (as they termed Mrs Faulkner). Unfortunately, Father Francis found out about their love affair, following a clandestine bicycle trip: the boys were removed to other lodgings and Ronald was forbidden to see or speak to Edith again until he was twenty-one. Edith was taken off to Cheltenham to stay with two elderly family friends, known by her as Uncle and Auntie Jessop.

ABOVE: *Ronald as an undergraduate*

RIGHT: *Edith with Auntie and Uncle Jessop*

The young couple were made miserable by this enforced separation, but Edith, after a while, fared better than Ronald. She was now living in comfort in a spacious house with several servants and could play to her heart's content on the grand piano. She also played the organ at the local Anglican church, relying, for small sums of money, on the village simpleton to pump the organ. This must have been an unrewarding job: after a while he would fall asleep at his post and would continue only when Edith, dismayed by the dismal sounds issuing from the instrument, pleaded with him to continue. From playing the organ she developed a back injury, and to her lasting regret had to give up playing; nor did she ever fully recover.

Although much happier in Cheltenham, Edith still suffered from having too much time on her hands and too little companionship with those her own age. Uncle Jessop appears to have been a martinet with a strong temper and a weak heart. He dominated his wife, who in turn begged Edith not to cross him. Edith said she would often work out her frustrations on the piano, playing something powerful and stirring, such as a Schubert Impromptu or a Beethoven sonata. She also spent hours copying music meticulously. One or two of her albums still remain, showing her taste ranging from classical music to the lighter ballads of the time.

So it was that during this period Edith became engaged to George Field, who was a farmer in Warwickshire and the brother of her schoolfriend, Molly.

Meanwhile, Ronald threw himself into his school activities and work, and won himself a scholarship to Oxford for the following year. During the summer holidays of 1911, before going up to Oxford for the first term, he and Hilary joined a party of family friends on a trip to Switzerland. Here, Ronald experienced mountain scenery for the first time in his life and it made such a deep impression on him that the icy peaks with their rock-falls and snowy crevasses were to lodge themselves in his imagination, later to reappear in various guises in *The Hobbit* and *The Lord of the Rings*.

That autumn Ronald went up to Exeter College, Oxford, with a minor scholarship. Exeter, one of the oldest colleges, is in the Turl, a narrow street off Broad Street. His rooms, in an unusual building called Swiss Cottage (now demolished), looked out onto the Turl: John had rooms in this very same building twenty-five years later.

At Christmas in 1911 Ronald returned to King Edward's School to take part in their production of 'The Rivals', earning himself excellent reviews for his portrayal of Mrs Malaprop.

J.R.R.T. with friends on the Aletsch Glacier

Back at college the next term it became clear that Ronald's great sociability and extra-curricular university activities were resulting in neglect of his studies. As well as playing rugby, and being a member of the college Essay Club, the Dialectical Society, and the Stapeldon (the college debating society), he also started his own club - the Apolausticks - devoted to 'self-indulgence'. Consequently, he found that his open exhibition and other grants did not fully cover his living expenses, and Father Francis had to continue contributing to his finances.

Cover of the Exeter College Magazine drawn by J.R.R.T.

King Edward's School

Musical :: and :: Dramatic :: Society

will present

"The Rivals"

By Richard Brinsley Sheridan,

.. IN ..

BIG SCHOOL.

On Thursday, December 21st, 1911,

At 7·30 p.m. Doors open at 7 p.m.

In aid of the School Cot Fund.

The Play will be acted by present members of the Society, assisted by J. R. R. TOLKIEN, and T. K. BARNSLEY.

Tickets may be obtained from R. Q. GILSON, or G. B. SMITH :—

RESERVED 2/-. UNRESERVED 1/-.

Tickets for members of the School Club :—

RESERVED 1/-. UNRESERVED 6d

Joe Wright

Having come up to study Latin and Greek – 'Greats' – Ronald found himself losing interest. He was attracted more to the Germanic languages, and to Comparative Philology, taught by Joe Wright, an ex-mill-hand who had taught himself to read and write, eventually becoming a Professor.

At about the same time Ronald also discovered Finnish and began to create another private language which would later emerge as 'Quenya' or 'High-elven'.

On 3 January 1913, Ronald turned twenty-one. He wrote immediately to Edith. She replied, informing him of her engagement. On receipt of her letter, he set out for Cheltenham at once to see her. Edith capitulated, ended her engagement to George Field and became formally engaged to Ronald. Their respective guardians were not enthusiastic, although Father Francis eventually gave his blessing. Uncle Jessop expressed concern about the young couple's future in a letter to Edith's guardian, Stephen Gateley:

'I have nothing to say against Tolkien, he is a cultured gentm.,
but his prospects are poor in the extreme, and when he will be in
a position to marry I cannot imagine. Had he adopted a
profession it would have been different.'

The letter holds considerable humorous irony for those of us reading it today!

Ronald now returned his attention to his academic work, passing his Honour Moderations, achieving an almost unprecedented 'alpha' in Comparative Philology. On the strength of this it was suggested that Ronald transfer to the English School, which he did at the start of the summer term in 1913. Earlier in the year he had sent Edith a postcard from Exeter College showing the dining hall. 'X' marked the spot where he sat.

Father Francis sometimes came to visit from Birmingham, once chaperoning Edith. She remembered the train stopping at Banbury and Father Francis insisting on buying Banbury cakes - the local delicacy - which were very greasy. The grease got everywhere and caused considerable confusion.

That same summer, Ronald took the job of escorting two young Mexican boys to France: a harrowing experience, for he witnessed the death of the boys' aunt in a traffic accident and had to deal with the funeral arrangements. There was, however, a lighter side to the holiday, for he had a thoroughly enjoyable time exploring Paris and later in life would entertain the family with his expert mimicry of the accents of Paris errand-boys and their gutter talk.

J.R.R.T. in Paris, 1913 (fifth from back on charabanc)

That same year, Ronald persuaded Edith to adopt the Catholic faith. When she did so, Uncle Jessop ordered her to leave his home at once. She found a rented house with her cousin, Jenny Grove, and her dog, Sam, in Warwick, and Ronald joined them there in June 1913. Jenny, known in the family as Auntie Ie, became a substitute mother to Edith and the nearest thing her four children had to a grandmother. Due to an accident in her youth she was only four feet eight inches in height, but she was a doughty character.

At the house in Warwick Edith had her own piano, which she played regularly until in old age arthritis made this too painful. Priscilla has this piano to this day. She also has the beautiful set of hand-painted Staffordshire china cherished by her mother all her life.

Edith's house at
15 Victoria Road, Warwick

The Great War broke out the following year. Ronald was still completing his degree at Oxford. In June 1915 he took his final examinations, gaining a First Class Honours degree. Immediately after this he took up a commission with the 13th Battalion of the Lancashire Fusiliers. Both our parents spoke feelingly of this time spent living in the shadow of war. They were married before Ronald was posted abroad on 22 March 1916, at the Catholic Church of St Mary Immaculate in Warwick, and spent their honeymoon at Clevedon in Somerset. Edith gave up the house in Warwick (with some regret) and settled in lodgings with Ronald and Jenny at Great Heywood in Staffordshire, near the training camp.

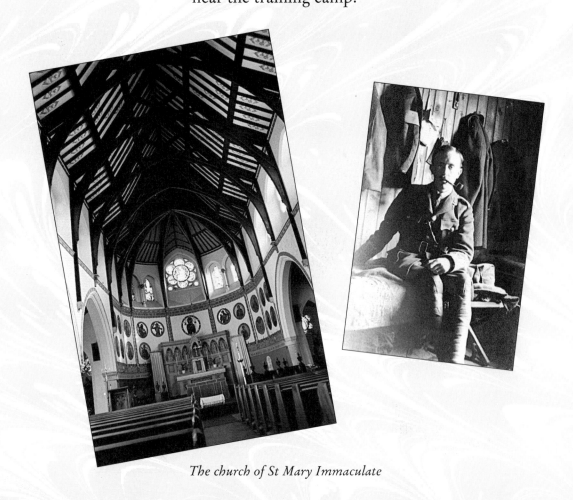

The church of St Mary Immaculate

38

On 2 June Ronald received the fateful telegram summoning him to Folkestone to embark for France on 5 June. The couple spent their last night together at the Plough & Harrow Hotel in Birmingham, where the family were to stay on one occasion many years later.

Ronald arrived at Calais on 6 June and all too soon the battalion were sent to the Front, to the Somme.

Like thousands of others, our mother longed for the messages Ronald sent. They arrived on official forms, and it was hard to tell much beyond the fact that the sender was then still alive. Because of this, our parents devised a private code of dots. Edith kept a large map of France on the wall and could gauge fairly well where Ronald was at any time. During this period she carried the added burden of being Hilary's next-of-kin: he suffered a number of minor shrapnel wounds while serving as a private in the Royal Warwickshire regiment, helping to carry supplies over the notorious Paschendael Ridge. Each time he was wounded Edith would receive a telegram . . .

Hilary Tolkien, 1914

Ronald probably survived his time in the trenches only because he caught trench fever in the latter part of the year and was sent home. In later years he would occasionally talk of being at the Front: of the horrors of the first German gas attack, of the utter exhaustion and ominous quiet after a bombardment, of the whining scream of the shells, and the endless marching, always on foot, through a devastated landscape, sometimes carrying the men's equipment as well as his own to encourage them to keep going. Years later he would compare these experiences with those of his son Michael, a soldier in the Second World War, who endured his share of horrors but was at least part of an army with motorised transport.

Some remarkable relics survive from that time: a trench map he drew himself; pencil-written orders to carry bombs to the 'fighting line'.

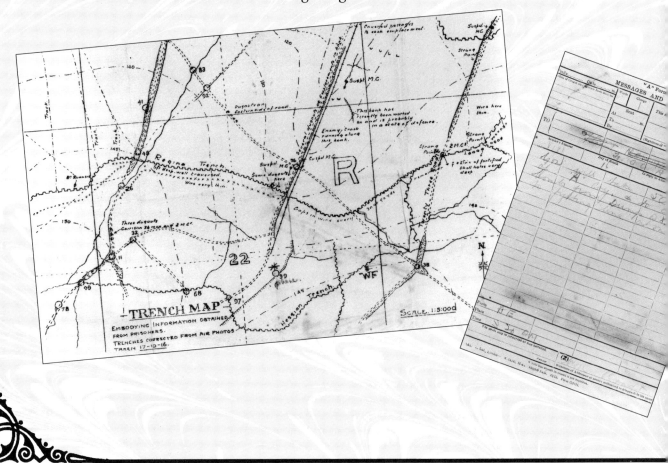

The loss of so many of his friends, both from school and university, remained a lifelong sadness. None did he mourn more than his old school friend, Geoffrey Smith, fellow member of the TCBS. Priscilla remembers visiting an old blind lady in Birmingham in the 1930s with our parents. With tears in her eyes the old lady said, 'You know, I lost both my boys in that war.' It was Mrs Smith: both Geoffrey and his brother had perished in the conflict.

ABOVE: *Ronald and Edith, 1917*
LEFT: *G.B. Smith*

During Ronald's long convalescence in 1917, John was born. The family took rooms in the Humberside village of Roos, near where Ronald was stationed.

When Ronald was demobilised after the Armistice he came back to Oxford, and the family, including Edith's cousin Jenny Grove, found rooms at 50 St John's Street with a Miss Mahon. She was a colourful character and a woman of some presence. Our parents would tell stories of how they would enter her kitchen with some trepidation to find piles of unwashed dishes mounting up towards the ceiling, and on top of such a pile a large cockerel looking down at them with an unnerving expression in its eye. John learned to walk in the nearby St John's College Gardens, which he regarded as his own, inviting visitors to come and see *his* garden.

Ronald started work as an assistant lexicographer on the Oxford English Dictionary. Begun in the 1880s by Sir James Murray, it was now under the editorship of Henry Bradley. J.R.R.T. loved seeking out words and their provenance, so the job suited him very well. He worked on the letter 'W': for example, the entry for 'walrus' is his! He never denied the story that when a critic of the OED once queried a derivation he had retorted angrily: 'The OED is me.'

walrus ('wɒlrəs). Also 8 walrus, wallross, *pl.* walrosses, 9 -russes. [probably a. Du. *walrus* (*walros*). Compare (i) LG. *walross*, G. *walross* (earlier also *walruss*, *walrusch*), Sw. hvalross, *valross* (*valruss*), Da. *hvalros* (earlier also *hvalrusk*), walrus; (ii) OE. *horschwæl*, early mod.G. *rosswal*, *russwal*, Norw. *russhval*, walrus, ? OFr. *rohal*, *rohart*, *rochal* (whence med.L. *rohanlum*, *-allum*) walrus-ivory; see RUEL.
The forms under (i) appear to be later than those under (ii) from which they perh. arose (? in Du.) by metathesis on some analogy such as that of Du. *walvisch* whale.
The interpretation of formation (ii) as 'horse-whale' (zoologically improbable) appears to be only one of the various popular etymologies that have influenced the forms of the word. Ultimately a confusion, either within or outside the Scandinavian languages, has perhaps taken place between ON. *hrosshvalr* a kind of whale, and *rosmhvalr* walrus. The latter is related obscurely to ON. *rosmall*, Norw. *rosmaal*, *rosmaar*, Da. *rosmær*, *-er*, *-ar* walrus, whence the scientific specific name *rosmarus*. See ROSMARINE². Some scholars have connected *rosm-* with ON., Icel. *rostungr* walrus, and assumed relationship of both with ON. *rauðr* RED. (Cf. RORQUAL and OHG. *ros(a)mo* redness.) This is zoologically possible, but it seems more likely that *rosm-* is a corruption of some non-Teut. word: cf. MORSE.]
1. The sea-horse, or morse (*Trichechus rosmarus*), a carnivorous pinniped marine mammal allied to the *Phocidae* (seals), and *Otariidae* (sea-lions), and chiefly distinguished by two tusks (exserted upper canine teeth). It inhabits the Arctic seas. A variety found in the N. Pacific has sometimes received the distinct specific name *obesus*.
[*c* **893** ÆLFRED *Oros.* I. i. §15 For þæm horschwælum, for ðæm hie habbað swiþe æþele ban on hiora toþum. **1655** O. WORM *Mus.* III. xv. 289 Animal..quod Anglis & Russis Walrus, aliis Mors, Danis & Islandis Rosmarus vocatur. **1693** RAY *Syn. Anim. Quadr.* etc. 191 Anglis Mors à Russis mutuato nomine. Belgis Walrus... The Morse or Sea-Horse.] **1728** J. WOODWARD *Catal. Fossils* II. *Foreign* II. 22 A Tusk of the Morse, or Walrous, call'd by some the Sea-Horse. **1752** HILL *Hist. Anim.* 555 The Phoca, with the canine teeth exerted. The Walrus. **1796** MORSE *Amer. Geog.* II. 75 The seals, walrosses, and cod, caught in the Russian seas, are likewise very important articles. **1833** SIR C. BELL *Hand* (1834) 109 The bones of the morse or walrus..are remarkably complete, if we consider the peculiar

Later that year they moved to 1 Alfred Street, and employed a cook-maid, much to Edith's delight. John remembers seeing the St Giles' Fair at that time, which then included wild animals. These were taken out for exercise early in the morning, and he recalls that as elephants were taken down Alfred Street, they blocked out the light as they passed the dining-room window. It was not possible for J.R.R.T. to keep his family on the part-time work offered by the Dictionary, so he began to make a foothold for himself in the University. Anglo-Saxon was expanding as a subject and some of the recently-founded women's colleges were looking for tutors in this field. He was interviewed by the head of St Hugh's: years later he described her as a formidable woman, dressed in the style of his grandmother, buttoned top-to-toe in an ankle-length dress. He remembered the severity of her expression as she enquired, 'Are you married, Mr Tolkien?', and her relief at his reply. Thus Ronald gained some employment tutoring her students.

ABOVE: *1 Alfred Street*

RIGHT: *Leeds University, c. 1920*

In 1921 J.R.R.T. got a post at Leeds University in the English Department and for the first few months the family, now numbering four - Michael having been born in Oxford in 1920 - lived at Hollybank, a house they rented from Miss Moseley, a niece of Cardinal Newman.

Hollybank

Then they moved to 11 St Marks Terrace, not far from the University, an area now demolished and built over. Then it was dingy and soot-covered. Chemicals in the air rotted the curtains within six months, and baby Michael was covered in smuts if he was left outside in his pram for any length of time; and Ronald found that he had to change his collar three times a day!

Edith, Michael and John on the steps of the house on St Marks Terrace, Leeds

John retains many memories of this time, especially the sound of trams rattling past at the end of the road; and a Christmas party for all the children of university staff when the Vice-Chancellor, dressed as Father Christmas, got stuck trying to come down the chimney, so that only a pair of waving legs showed until he crashed to the ground with a tremendous pile of parcels. As a result of this party, both John and Michael caught measles, a fact that is noted in mother's account book at that time! Mother's accounts were always meticulous, and they had to be since the Leeds post did not pay well, as can be seen from the entry of J.R.R.T.'s salary in the Leeds University Register. J.R.R.T. spent many weeks each summer marking examination scripts from other universities to supplement the family income.

Feb. 26th 1922	Cash brought forward from last Week.	Feb. 27th Monday	28th Tuesday	Mar. 1st Wednesday	2nd Thursday	3rd Friday	4th Saturday	Totals and Balance.
DAILY RECEIPTS.	9 16 10							
Baker		6	1.2	7	6	6.8	2.10	5.7
Butcher					1.2		4	8.2
Fishmonger & Poulterer			8.6	2.0 2.10		9 2.6		2.9 16.8
Grocer					6	2.0	2.10	6
Cheesemonger						2.0		
Greengrocer						2.0	1.1	4.8
Milkman		1.5 6	8	1.6	9	1.2	1.10	4.6 9
Wine, Beer, &c.						1.0		1.0
Laundress, &c.								
Holidays								
Coals, Gas, Water, &c.								
Rent, Taxes, &c.								
Glass, China, &c.								
Hardware & Repairs				9				9
Dress, Draper, &c.								
Shoemaker								
Tailor & Hatter								
Education								
Doctor & Chemist		1.3			6	2.6		4.3
Donations & Charities								
Garden & Stable								
Stationer						1.0		1.0
Travelling			2.6.8	2.5.3 0				3
Wages							5.6	4.11.8
Sundries					J.1.0.0			0.0 5.6
Total of each Day's Payments		3.8	2.17.0	2.13.5	1.3.5	16.7	15.5	8.9.6
				£58.14.11				1.7.4
				8.9.6 Cash in hand at end of Week carried to next page				
				£67.4.5 Total for 9 weeks				£1.7.4

9th WEEK.

MEMORANDA FOR THE WEEK.

Feb.
27th Monday — Michael cut 11th tooth — 2nd Canine.

SHROVE Tuesday 28th — Mary left. Went to the Dentist.
Royal Wedding!

ASH Wednesday Mar. 1st — Cooked my first dinner!

2nd Thursday — Cooked a nice dinner! Started a cold. Michael also.

3rd Friday — Very bad cold. Unable to go with R. to their dining

4th Saturday — Cooked my 1st big dinner! Mrs Brodetsky came in.
(★ vig)

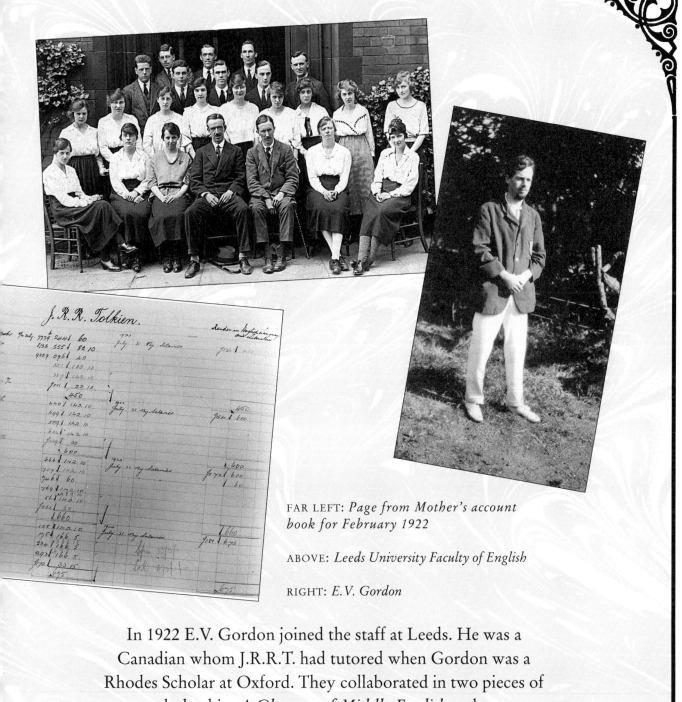

FAR LEFT: *Page from Mother's account book for February 1922*

ABOVE: *Leeds University Faculty of English*

RIGHT: *E.V. Gordon*

In 1922 E.V. Gordon joined the staff at Leeds. He was a Canadian whom J.R.R.T. had tutored when Gordon was a Rhodes Scholar at Oxford. They collaborated in two pieces of scholarship: *A Glossary of Middle English* and an edition of the Middle English poem *Sir Gawain and the Green Knight*. Together they helped to found the Viking Club amongst undergraduates, which besides drinking, singing and reading sagas, translated nursery rhymes into Anglo-Saxon.

Christopher was born in 1924, and in the same year J.R.R.T. was made a professor and appointed to the Chair of English Language; the family moved to Darnley Road, a three-storey house on the outskirts of the city.

John's earliest memories of Ronald as a storyteller go back to Darnley Road during 1924 and 1925: when John was unable to sleep Ronald would sit upon the bed and tell him wonderful stories, which he never wrote down.

ABOVE: *Darnley Road*

LEFT: *Edith and baby Christopher*

UNIVERSITY INTELLIGENCE

THE appointment of four new Professors from the University Staff has caused great pleasure among the undergraduates. Professor Tolkien has been appointed to the Chair of English Language. He has held the post of Reader in Language at Leeds University since 1920, but he is well known also at the University of Oxford as one of the most noted specialists of our times in English Language. The great distinction of his academic career has been followed by valuable researches, which have won for him an eminent authority in English Philology and kindred sciences. Mr. Tolkien is esteemed highly by all the students, particularly by the School of English, where he is extremely popular.

The earliest written story dates from September 1925 when the family took a holiday at Filey, on the east coast, a town they had visited once before in 1922. They rented a cottage high above the seafront and John remembers that it was dark before his bedtime, and he was excited to see the full moon rising out of the sea, producing a 'moonpath' across the water. When Michael lost his little lead dog, which he carried everywhere, on the beach, Ronald wrote a story called *Roverandum* about a little dog sent by a wizard up the moonpath to meet the Man in the Moon. During this visit there was a terrible storm that smashed the bathing-huts and brought the sea up into the town. Ronald sat by the bed all night because we thought the roof was going to come off!

In 1925 J.R.R.T. was offered the Professorship of Anglo-Saxon in Oxford and early the following year our family moved down from Leeds to a new house in North Oxford - 22 Northmoor Road.

Unlike most professors, Ronald did not have rooms in college: instead he commuted regularly between home and Pembroke College in the centre of town. He became a familiar figure cycling at deliberate speed down the Banbury Road on his exceptionally high-seated bicycle, often wearing his academic cap and gown! He must have been a sufficiently unusual sight to have one morning caught the excited attention of a young boy, whom he heard saying loudly, 'Look, Mum, a singer!' Because of this, he spent more time at home than most fathers, and we usually shared his company at meal-times.

Family tea party,
22 Northmoor Road, May 1928

Ronald and Christopher, 1928

J.R.R.T. lectured several times a week during the university term which took up most of his time and energy. Although required to give a minimum of 36 lectures or classes a year, he was extremely assiduous in teaching his beloved subject, and in 1927 he gave 136 classes and lectures! Throughout the 1930s he continued to give at least twice the statutory number, considerably more than his colleagues. Another large area of responsibility was examining for the Oxford English Faculty, which he continued to do right up to his retirement.

Christopher, May 1928

Merton College

J.R.R.T.'s lectures - especially those on the great Old English poem *Beowulf* and the famous Middle English poem *Sir Gawain and the Green Knight* - continued to build on his reputation for generating excitement and interest in his student audience. One former student, the writer J.I.M. Stewart, said, 'He would turn a lecture room into a mead hall in which he was the bard and we were the feasting, listening guests.' On the basis of this reputation he was asked to deliver his famous lecture 'Beowulf: The Monster and the Critics' at the British Academy in 1936. Priscilla remembers the very unusual event of both our parents travelling down to London for the day. They came home with the tale of having hailed a taxi driver who, ignorant of the British Academy, took them instead to the Royal Academy. They eventually reached their destination, with only minutes to spare!

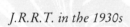

J.R.R.T. in the 1930s

He was also notorious for his remarkable inaudibility and the way he would move quickly from one idea to the next! In an article entitled 'My Hero' in *The Independent* magazine (March 1989) Dr Robert Burchfield, a distinguished scholar and lexicographer of the Oxford Dictionary, recorded: 'I was entranced by the arguments that he presented to largely bewildered audiences of undergraduates. . . By the third week of term his small band

of true followers remained. And I was always one of them . . .
I shall continue to look back in gratitude and reverence to the
puckish fisherman who drew me into his glittering net.'
In 1929 our neighbours, the bookseller Basil Blackwell and
his family, moved out of number twenty; and our family
decided to move in over the fence. We all became deeply
attached to this house, which was our home for seventeen
years: for Priscilla, who was born in 1929, it was the scene of
her entire childhood.

ABOVE: *20 Northmoor Road, 1930*

RIGHT: *Family party, 20 Northmoor Road,
March 1930*

20 Northmoor Road was as much loved for its garden as for the house. John and Ronald worked at landscaping and redesigning the garden over many years, turning the rather decrepit tennis court at the top into a vegetable garden: an important asset during the war years that were to follow. Over the years we lived there the trees planted by the Blackwells grew almost to forest height. In a side garden, Edith had an aviary, in which budgerigars, canaries and other exotic birds lived during the summer months, being taken indoors for the winter. In war-time, the aviary was turned into a hen-house and the fowls and their eggs became an important part of the household economy. Priscilla retains a strong memory of Ronald at that time cleaning out the hens, all the while smoking a large and pungent pipe.

Ronald and Priscilla, Summer 1930

From the outside the house looks deceptively large and remarkably unchanged to this day. The rooms were not large, but there were so many small ones that each member of the family had his or her own room.

The most exciting room was J.R.R.T.'s study, which was never out of bounds except when he had students with him. The walls were lined with books from floor to ceiling, and it contained a great black lead stove, the source of considerable drama every day: first thing in the morning Ronald would light and draw it, then become distracted by other business, from which he would be aroused by shouts from the neighbours or the postman that the chimney was on fire, black smoke pouring out of it. During the 1930s there was a fire at the house, which originated in the loft. J.R.R.T. was sitting in Convocation (the University parliament) at the time, waiting to give a speech in front of the Vice Chancellor. He was full of nervous anticipation, when a uniformed porter came up and whispered loudly to him, 'Your 'ouse is on fire. You 'ad better go 'ome!' Luckily, Edith had caught it just in time to prevent serious damage.

The study was very much the centre of Ronald's home life, and the centre of his study was his desk. Over the years the top of his desk continued to show familiar landscapes: his dark brown wooden tobacco jar, a Toby jug containing pipes and a large bowl into which the ash from his pipe was regularly knocked out. We also vividly remember a row of coloured Quink and Stevenson inks, and sets of sealing-wax in different shades to match his large supply of stationery.

DRAWINGS FOR "THE HOBBIT"
by J R R TOLKIEN
· AN EXHIBITION ·
to celebrate the fiftieth anniversary of its publication

Bilbo comes to the Huts of the Raft-elves

24 FEBRUARY TO 23 MAY 1987
SCHOLA NATURALIS PHILOSOPHIAE · OLD LIBRARY QUADRANGLE
BODLEIAN LIBRARY · OXFORD
MONDAY TO FRIDAY 9 TO 5 · SATURDAY 9 TO 12.30 · ADMISSION FREE

There were also wonderful boxes of Koh-i-Noor coloured pencils, and tubes of paint with magical names like Burnt Sienna, Gamboge and Crimson Lake. Priscilla clearly recalls her father showing her how beautifully Chinese White could be used when he was painting 'Bilbo Comes to the Huts of the Raft-elves' (his favourite painting and the one chosen by the Bodleian for the poster advertising their exhibition of his work in 1987 to celebrate the fiftieth anniversary of the first publication of *The Hobbit*).

57

He demonstrated how white could be an addition to a painting, rather than an absence of colour. He was also experimenting with Indian inks at this time, for the many black and white pictures he drew to accompany the book, such as 'Beorn's Hall'. Later, in the 1940s, when he was hoping to illustrate *The Lord of the Rings*, he became more interested in using coloured chalks and experimenting with coloured papers. During their years at Northmoor Road, Ronald would invite John, Michael and Christopher to sit on the study floor and there he would read chapters of *The Hobbit* to them. Each chapter was an evening's entertainment: this period took the story up to 'Riddles in the Dark'. Christopher was always much concerned with the consistency of the story and on one occasion (as he recounted in his foreword to the 50th Anniversary edition of *The Hobbit*) interrupted: 'Last time, *you* said Bilbo's front door was blue, and *you* said Thorin had a golden tassel on his hood, but you've just said that Bilbo's front door was green, and the tassel on Thorin's hood was silver'; at which Ronald exclaimed 'Damn the boy!' and strode across the room to make a note.

Christmas was always an exciting time. As children, we would write letters to Father Christmas for weeks before his arrival, and the letters that we put out always disappeared mysteriously. On Christmas Eve the excitement would become unbearable: after tea it was time to go up and choose one of Ronald's woollen winter stockings - a serious ritual - and we made our choices with great deliberation as to the relative size of each sock. Going to sleep was always very difficult.

On Christmas morning - in common with thousands of other children - we would be allowed to open our stockings and unwrap our carefully chosen presents; but for us there was an extra element: every year we would receive a letter from Father Christmas himself, postmarked 'the North Pole', complete with a North Pole stamp! It would be in elaborate handwriting telling us of news at the North Pole, and the licensed fooleries of the Polar Bear were our especial delight, together with the coloured picture accompanying the letter.

We had no idea for many years that anyone other than Father Christmas was responsible for these wonderful letters.

Often, Ronald would bribe the postman into delivering them with the regular post: at other times we would find sooty footmarks around the fireplace . . . So precious was this tradition that the secret of Father Christmas's actual identity

was carefully preserved over the years, and Priscilla was able to continue to exchange letters with him and hang up her stocking long after her brothers had left this delight of childhood behind them. The final letter and picture was received in 1943, dark with references to 'this horrible war'.

The letters and pictures were carefully preserved in a large brown envelope which Ronald kept in a corner of his desk in the study. Here they were to remain as a shared family memory, until they were edited after his death by Christopher's wife, Baillie, and published in a beautiful volume under the title *The Father Christmas Letters*.

Other shared family memories include the various holidays
we had together. In 1927 and 1928 John remembers going to
Lyme Regis in Dorset, where Father Francis had taken
Ronald and Hilary as boys. John has a few isolated
recollections of these holidays: Father Francis (who joined
us on one of these trips) producing a pile of marshmallows
on top of an ant-hill as if by magic; father, curious about the
workings, breaking the cuckoo-clock in the lodging house,
causing considerable annoyance to the landlady...

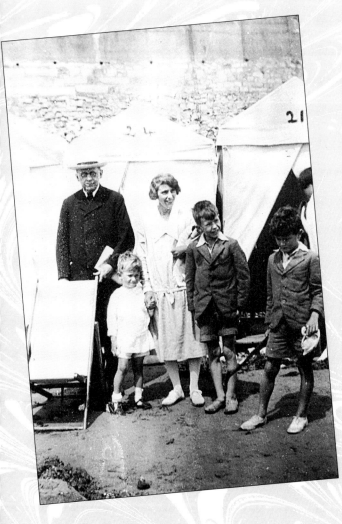

ABOVE: *Lyme Regis, 1928*

LEFT: *The family with Father
Francis, Lyme Regis, August 1928*

In 1931 the family went on a spring holiday to Milford-on-Sea, where Michael's godfather, Father Gus Emery, lived. He had a bungalow with a chapel in the house, which served as the local Catholic church. This was Priscilla's first visit to the seaside (she was barely two years old). John remembers walking with his father along the shingle spit to Hurst Castle, a fort jutting out into the Solent, where Charles I had been imprisoned.

In 1932 we spent a month at Lamorna Cove, a beautiful spot on the Cornish coast beyond Penzance. We shared this holiday with Charles and Agnes Wrenn and their daughter Carola. It was a delightful, carefree holiday, with walks as far as Land's End, bathing in the cove, and complete isolation from the outside world.

BELOW: *Edith and Priscilla, Milford-on-Sea, April 1931*

RIGHT: *Lamorna Cove, 1932*

Later that year Ronald purchased our first car - a dignified Morris known as Old Jo, followed shortly by an updated model known as Jo 2. There was no such thing as a driving test then, so Ronald was able to drive, but not always safely: as might be guessed from his tale of Mister Bliss! The car - or rather the combination of the car and Ronald as driver - produced some adventures; notably an early outing to visit his brother Hilary on his small fruit farm near Evesham (where Uncle Hilary remained until a few months before his death in 1976). This was no great distance away, yet in the space of a very few miles, not only did he drive off the road and demolish a wall,

Jo 2

but also managed to get a puncture. It was not easy in those days to find a garage to mend it, and what with the accident and the long wait, only part of the family was willing to make the return trip in the car! Celebratory visits were sometimes made to take tea at country inns, like The Roof Tree at Woodstock (now long since gone), The White Hart at Dorchester (now a very grand restaurant) and The George at Sandford-on-Thames. More often these expeditions were in search of wildlife: one year we had the excitement of finding a rare Bee Orchid in the countryside around Worminghall, the area that was to become the setting for the Little Kingdom in J.R.R.T.'s story *Farmer Giles of Ham.*

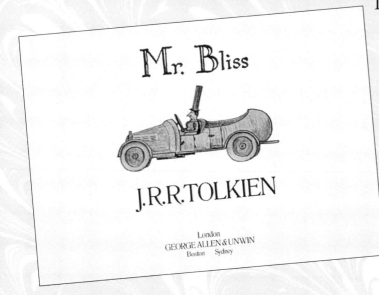

Mr. Bliss

J.R.R.TOLKIEN

London
GEORGE ALLEN & UNWIN
Boston   Sydney

63

From 1934 onwards family holidays became important annual events, and in that year we first began to spend the first two weeks of September, before the boys went back to school, in Sidmouth, Devon. Sidmouth was then a small seaside town with a fashionable past. It spread out from a core of elegant Regency and Victorian houses, but its hinterland consisted of the remains of the original fishing village, now somewhat poor and dilapidated.

Ronald would drive Jo 2, weighed down with luggage, squeezing in himself at the last possible moment. He would be surrounded by large numbers of Priscilla's soft toys, which she insisted should share the holiday: on one trip someone asked him if he was a travelling salesman in teddy bears!

ABOVE: *Priscilla's 'family'*

RIGHT: *Edith and John, Sidmouth, 5 September 1938*

Edith would travel down with Christopher and Priscilla by train, there being no room for them in the car; and John and Michael would cycle down, taking two or three days over the journey with frequent stops for heady West Country cider on the way - which they sometimes slept off on the grass verges!

Between 1934 and 1937 we stayed at a house called 'Aurora' in the older part of the town, settling down to a routine of swimming, sitting on the beach, shopping in town, playing clock-golf on the green opposite and making expeditions to more distant beaches to collect beautiful, rare shells like cowries.

During our Sidmouth holiday in 1938 tension over the Czech crisis was at its height: in 1939 the outbreak of war meant that we had to cancel our booking. We would never go there again as a family, although Priscilla and our parents were to make other visits to Sidmouth in later years. (Michael, who was appointed to coastal defence in Sidmouth in 1941, persuaded his commanding officer to test the in situ guns there. The results were disastrous: the concrete gun emplacements were inadequate, and most of the guns collapsed!)

Our last holiday as a family: Christopher, Priscilla, Michael and our parents. Weston-Super-Mare, 1940

Parts of J.R.R.T.'s life at this time were in many ways separate to his life with his family, including his friendship with Clive Staples Lewis, then a young don at Magdalen College. From 1931 onwards the two of them were prominent members of an informal gathering of friends, known as 'The Inklings', together with Lewis's brother Warnie, Owen Barfield, Hugo Dyson and J.R.R.T.'s and C. S. Lewis's doctor, Dr Havard (known affectionately as UQ - Useless Quack!). (Later, during the Second World War, Charles Williams, who worked for the Oxford University Press in London, was evacuated to Oxford and joined the group.)

The 'Bird & Baby'

Membership of The Inklings was fluid and shifting, and the Tuesday meetings were especially informal. These were held late in the morning at the Eagle & Child in St Giles (known more often as 'The Bird & Baby': there is now a small permanent exhibition in the back part of the pub to commemorate the group). Whoever turned up would engage in a multitude of subjects depending on what was topical or of interest to them at that time. John attended some of the meetings if he was at home on holiday in the 1940s. He remembers one such discussion concerning the gender of trees; how some are either male or female and rely on proximity for fertilisation - like the yew.

A few days later while walking along St Cross Road John saw C. S. Lewis ahead of him, beating the yews with his stick to discover which would give out pollen, exclaiming, 'Got you!' when he met with success!

C.S. Lewis

The Thursday evening meetings were held in Lewis's rooms at Magdalen College and would commence when a reasonable number had arrived. Someone would produce a manuscript and start to read. Lewis's *Screwtape Letters* began as a weekly reading for The Inklings, as did chapters of *The Hobbit* during the 1930s; and chapters of *The Lord of the Rings* during the 1940s. Discussion, praise or criticism would follow and then the meeting would drift into a variety of subjects until a late hour. Christopher also attended the meetings when he returned to Oxford at the end of the war. The group dissolved in 1954 when Lewis left Magdalen for Cambridge.

Both of our parents had a gift for enduring friendships. Edith's oldest friend was Mabel Sheaf, with whom she had been at Dresden House School. They met at the age of fourteen and stayed in close contact over the years, despite marriage and children, and geographical distance. Priscilla remembers visits to the Sheafs' farm at Hinton-on-the-Green during the 1930s and even as a child Priscilla was aware of the desperate struggle against poverty the family were facing in the Great Agricultural Depression; but after the war the family emigrated to New Zealand. Edith realised she would almost certainly never see her old schoolfriend again, but nevertheless the pair kept up a regular correspondence right up until Edith's death in 1971. Mabel died the following year.

Many of our parents' friends were originally J.R.R.T.'s students. One of these was to become a close family friend: Meredith Thompson (known by us as 'Merry Tom') who had come from the University of Winnipeg in the 1930s to study at Oriel College and to

Mabel Sheaf outside 'The Manor'

work with J.R.R.T. He was later to become a distinguished academic, holding a Chair in English in Los Angeles and at Vancouver, where he still lives. Over the years he has taken some of the best photos in the family collection.

Another student who was to become a friend was Simonne d'Ardenne, a Belgian medieval philologist who studied Middle English with J.R.R.T. during the 1930s, and who was later to become Professor of English at the University of Liège. For a time she lived with us and acted as a sort of unofficial aunt. Then Simonne returned to Belgium and she and J.R.R.T. exchanged many letters about the state of Europe and the imminent approach of war. We heard nothing from, or about, her until we received a message from the International Red Cross in 1943 to say that she and her family were alive and well. The village where she lived with her elderly father was close to the German border and had been occupied by German troops. She had taken great risks helping Allied Servicemen to escape, once driving an RAF man, disguised as a peasant, through the village in her horse and cart: although confronted by a lorry carrying SS troops, they were both taken to be local people and were not stopped.

'Merry Tom'

In the 1950s J.R.R.T. visited Simonne at her home - originally her family's hunting lodge in their days of aristocratic wealth - in the remote Ardennes. She continued to correspond with the family, and was especially close to Priscilla, up until her death in 1986. She entrusted to Priscilla a great bundle of letters she had received from J.R.R.T. over a period of forty years.

Simonne d'Ardenne

Many of them give a unique insight into his thoughts: in one letter dated 13 March 1936 he wrote: 'The political situation is dreadful . . . I have the greatest sympathy with Belgium - which is about the right size of any country! I wish my own were bounded still by the seas of the Tweed, and the walls of Wales . . . we folk do at least know something of mortality and eternity and when Hitler (or a Frenchman) says 'Germany (or France) must live for ever' we know that he lies.' Another, dated 23 December 1954, mentions the cost of newly experienced fame: 'The Book (*The Lord of the Rings*) continues to sell astonishingly, and to receive tremendous praise, and the opposite. But, my dear, I am so dreadfully tired.' And, finally an extract from one letter dated 27 December 1971, a few weeks after Edith's death: 'I am faced with celebrations of my eightieth birthday, which alas! have now little attraction for me, but I must endeavour to meet with a little of the gallant and gay courage which Edith had in such full measure.'

But of all those friends who were originally J.R.R.T.'s pupils, perhaps Elaine Griffiths had the most unique part to play in our family's life. She became a close family friend, often taking Priscilla to exciting teas in Oxford, where she lives to this day. Through her connection with a member of the Allen & Unwin staff in the 1930s the manuscript of *The Hobbit* came to the notice of the publishers, who expressed great interest in the story. By dint of much hard work J.R.R.T. then put the incomplete manuscript in order, so that it could be published in 1937. In 1938 he received a literary prize for the Best Children's Story of the Year. A somewhat poignant memory is of him opening the letter at the breakfast table and passing the enclosed cheque for fifty pounds - a formidable sum in those days - to Edith, so that she could pay an outstanding doctor's bill with it.

Elaine Griffiths

The years just before the war, and the early wartime years, were a transitional time for our family: for the older children were moving away to make their own lives. From 1936 to 1939 John was at J.R.R.T.'s old college - Exeter College - and took his finals in the summer before the outbreak of war. Having decided on his vocation he travelled to Rome that November to study and train for the priesthood. It was an exciting and disturbed time. Although Italy had not yet entered the war, she was an ally of Germany and the number of German troops in Rome gradually increased until it became clear that it was not safe to be an English student in the city. After a five-day train journey via Paris, John caught the last boat to leave Le Havre and arrived safely back in Britain, much to our relief, since we had been listening closely to radio reports. Following a brief spell in the Lake District, the College settled for six years at Stonyhurst in Lancashire. John was ordained priest at the Church of St Gregory and Augustine in North Oxford in February 1946.

John serving the Rector

In contrast, Michael and Christopher joined the armed forces. Michael, who had been studying at Trinity College, enlisted with the Army and saw active service defending aerodromes in the Battle of Britain, and later in France, and over Germany. He was invalided out of the Army and returned to Oxford in 1944 to complete his degree. Christopher, who also went to Trinity, left to join the RAF in 1942 and trained to be a fighter pilot in South Africa, his father's homeland, returning after the war to finish his degree.

Priscilla was still at school, and life at home carried on for her as normally as possible despite the war. Edith struggled to keep the big house going with little or no domestic help and severe food-rationing - eked out somewhat by the tennis-court vegetable patch and eggs from the hens we kept in the garden. Our parents celebrated their Silver Wedding anniversary in 1941 with a modest supper party, which included Hugo Dyson and C. S. Lewis. Of the four children only Priscilla was able to attend.

Edith's huge Pye radio was of central importance at this time for news bulletins. We also heard with disturbing regularity the rasping voice of Lord Haw-Haw, who began his propaganda broadcasts with the words, 'Germany calling . . .'

Michael, August 1940

J.R.R.T. strove to combine his teaching with his extra duties of Air Raid Warden and member of the Firewatching Service. Oxford was not bombed: however, Priscilla remembers J.R.R.T.'s description of an ever-increasing fiery glow over the horizon one night when he was working late, as was his habit. The next day we heard that Coventry, only forty miles away, had been devastated by German incendiary raids.

The Examination Schools became a military hospital and the University had to remove to the Taylorian Institute. Pembroke College was partly taken over by the Ministry of Agriculture (at lunch one day Ronald reported that a notice on the College Lodge now read: PESTS: FIRST FLOOR) as well as the Army: J.R.R.T. and

Our hens at 20 Northmoor Road, during the War

the other dons and under-graduates had to retreat into the remaining space. On one occasion, while mounting his bicycle outside the college the basket capsized, spilling the contents. Within seconds the street appeared to be running with blood. Alerted by sounds of anger and distress a young Army officer appeared on the scene and sympathised with J.R.R.T.'s accident: 'Bad show, sir, losing all your vinegar like that.' There was an explosive response. 'Vinegar? It was a very rare College port!!' The young man was driven into rapid retreat.

For much of the time during the war years J.R.R.T was writing his new work - the one his publishers had been pressing him to produce to follow up his great success with *The Hobbit*. Priscilla remembers when she was about fourteen and only able to type with two fingers, typing out early chapters of *The Lord of the Rings*, her intense excitement at the outset of the story and her terror of the Black Riders' pursuit of the hobbits as they left the Shire. At that stage she had no idea how the story would develop, or end. She can also recall the thud of J.R.R.T.'s old Hammond typewriter as he typed out the complete manuscript, being unable to afford the luxury of a professional typist. The Hammond was a splendid-looking machine with twin castle-like turrets that operated the upper-case keys, and a wooden frame and lid which made it enormously heavy.

Priscilla, 1954. Photo taken by Meredith Thompson

Ronald kept in very close imaginative contact with Christopher during 1944 and 1945 when Christopher was stationed in South Africa. In these letters (many of which appear in the volume of letters published after J.R.R.T.'s death) he sent Christopher regular instalments of the book as he wrote them, as well as discussing the ideas and problems he was encountering. Here is an extract of one letter written to Christopher on 29 November 1944: 'Here is a small consignment of The Ring: the last two chapters that have been written, and the end of the Fourth Book of the great romance in which you will see that . . . I have got the hero into such a fix that not even an author will be able to extract him without labour and difficulty. Lewis was moved almost to tears by the last chapter. All the same, I chiefly want to hear what you think, as for a long time I have written with you in mind.'

(In his later years Ronald shared much of his literary and philological imagination with Christopher, himself an Anglo-Saxon and Middle English scholar and a philologist. After Ronald's death Christopher was to carry out the immense task of editing J.R.R.T.'s vast, unfinished work, *The Silmarillion*, for publication in 1977; and subsequently he undertook an enormous study of the development of J.R.R.T.'s literary imagination, now reaching nine volumes: *The History of Middle-earth*.)

Christopher training in South Africa

Family group, 20 Northmoor Road, 1945

In 1945, after nearly twenty years as Professor of Anglo-Saxon, J.R.R.T. was appointed Merton Professor of English Language and Literature, with especial responsibility for Middle English up to 1500, a post which he held until his retirement in 1959. It soon became clear that the large family house at 20 Northmoor Road had to be given up now that the household was reduced to three. We all regarded the leave-taking as the end of our childhood and the end of a long chapter in family history. Our parents sold the house and moved in 1947 to a small terraced house in Manor Road, off Holywell Street in the centre of Oxford, a house which belonged to Merton College. In postwar Oxford there was a desperate shortage of housing and although our parents were thankful to have a College house they found both house

Ronald, Priscilla, Christopher and Edith, 3 Manor Road, 1949

and garden cramped and claustrophobic after the spaciousness of 20 Northmoor Road. Priscilla lived here with her parents until 1950, by which time she was an undergraduate at Lady Margaret Hall. All the family were relieved when a beautiful seventeenth and eighteenth century College house became vacant in Holywell Street, enabling Ronald, Edith and Priscilla to move to number 99. The house had a small step up from the street and lay back at an angle, looking, as Christopher remarked at the time, like someone leaning back after a good dinner. Its small garden contained a hawthorn tree that attracted nuthatches and tree creepers, and the high wall at the back, dividing it from the gardens of New College, was part of the medieval wall of the city. We were very much aware at the time that Oxford was a city of bells: the many churches and college chapels in the area had an idiosyncratic attitude to time and it would often take a quarter of an hour before the different hourly chimes were finished!

99 Holywell

Sadly, despite its lovely surroundings, this house did not prove to be the ideal setting for Ronald and Edith at this stage in their lives. Post-war Oxford was growing rapidly and Holywell Street had become a major traffic route across the city. Our parents had no defence against the noise this created and felt they must move again; so, with all four children now grown up and living away from home, Ronald and Edith decided to move up the hill to Headington, to 76 Sandfield Road. This was a modest, compact house with a pleasant garden, where they were to remain for the next fifteen years, until 1968. A plaque records this fact on the front of the house.

During this time the family was extending into a third generation, and as well as regular visits from their own children, our parents now also grew close to Michael's two elder children, Michael and Joan, and Christopher's eldest son, Simon.

LEFT: *Ronald and Edith with their grandson,*
Simon, at 99 Holywell, 1963

RIGHT: *Christopher, Baillie, baby Adam,*
Ronald and John, April 1969

In college life J.R.R.T. found Merton the antithesis of Pembroke: there were many younger dons with growing families, and wives and children were frequently seen in the college, which was rare at that time. There was, however, one survivor of older days: the distinguished classical scholar Professor Garrod. As a Fellow of the College for almost thirty years he was by this time a legendary figure, often seen crossing the Fellows' Quadrangle with his dog. As a young man during the First World War he had been accosted, while reading a book in Blackwell's, by an angry woman who demanded to know why he was not at the front fighting for the defence of civilisation. 'Madam,' he replied, not lifting his head from the book, 'I *am* civilisation.' Over the years J.R.R.T. achieved a humorous tolerance of the older man's idiosyncrasies.

Most important of all, J.R.R.T. had the pleasure of seeing two very old friends being appointed to the college: Hugo Dyson, and Neville Coghill, an old friend from his early days teaching at Oxford, who became the other Professor of English.

Professor Garrod

Now at last J.R.R.T. had a college base, with a spacious room in the beautiful seventeenth century Fellows' Quad overlooking Christ Church Meadows.

J.R.R.T. took a great interest in the annual Boat Races - Eights Week - which were held with great pageantry towards the end of May. (Priscilla remembers as a child the excitement of seeing all the flags flying on the way down the Broad Walk through Christ Church Meadows to the river, and its decorated barges crowded with expectant spectators craning their necks to see the boats with their different coloured oars coming up the river.) J.R.R.T. retained a strong affection for his undergraduate college, Exeter, and Priscilla remembers his conflict of loyalties when Exeter were rowing against Pembroke: whilst having tea with us once on the Pembroke barge he shouted for their opponents! The college barges were a delightful sight in pre-war days; but during the war they sadly fell into disrepair and were replaced by permanent brick boat-houses.

Eights Week continues today but with less pageantry. However, the view looking back across the Meadow towards Merton is as it was when our father's room with its lofty window framed it for him during his years at the College. (He was much distressed when this most unravished part of Oxford was threatened by plans to construct the inner ring road: fortunately, in the end the plans were changed.)

Eights Week

Merton College

Over the years at Merton J.R.R.T. served on various college committees, and for a while as Sub-Warden, which involved going with the Warden and Estates Bursar on a 'Progress' to view the College's extensive properties, in particular farmlands in Leicestershire and Lincolnshire. This gave him interesting insights into College administration in the early post-war years when rationing was still in force. It was a revelation to him how much more food there was available in the country and he thoroughly enjoyed meeting the farmers and experiencing their practical appreciation! Priscilla remembers him bringing home a magnificent ham, which made for a feast the like of which the family had not seen since before the war. He also served on the College Wine Committee, which gave him the pleasurable opportunity to extend his knowledge and appreciation of wine, and he was for a while Steward of Common Room, which involved him in keeping the master key of the College cellar. He once went away on holiday, taking the key with him in his pocket. A considerable crisis followed!

There was a considerable difference between his sophisticated taste in wine and his dislike of foreign or 'messed about' food. He attended many college dinners over the years and increasingly his antipathy towards French food and culture became more pronounced . In the last few months of his life he went to a dinner in Oxford which featured a traditional English Saddle of Mutton as the main course. On the telephone to Priscilla the next day he recounted the evening's pleasures. Then he lowered his voice and said, 'Do you know, for a few hours I could really believe that France didn't exist!'

He enjoyed warm relationships with the college's domestic staff. He was their champion, often arguing that they should enjoy better working conditions. We particularly remember one incident from this time: even at Christmas the college never closed altogether. One year Ronald found that a young porter had volunteered to remain on duty throughout the Christmas period because he was a single man, thus enabling all the other porters to enjoy the festivities with their families.

So on Christmas Day Ronald went down to the college to take the young porter, Mr Ramage, a bottle of wine. When he arrived he found Mr Ramage deep in study: he was preparing to apply for admission to the University. He later succeeded in his purpose and went on to read English at Balliol College.

The publication of *The Lord of the Rings* in 1954-5 was a turning point in J.R.R.T.'s life. His literary fame grew steadily and brought him great pleasure (once, while paying by cheque in a Dublin bookshop, the delighted bookseller responded excitedly, 'And is it the Lord of the Rings himself now that I am addressing?') but at times it also brought the annoyance of unwanted intrusions on his privacy.

Compared with the slow though steady following of *The Hobbit, The Lord of the Rings* soon made a great impact on readers all over the world, and translations included Japanese and Hebrew editions. In 1957 he received the medal of the Royal Society of Literature; in the same year he was somewhat bemused to receive a cigarette lighter in the form of a space rocket, awarded to him at the International Fantasy Congress.

Time was drawing on. In 1959 Edith became 70 and Ronald 67. After over forty years of holding Professorships in Oxford and lecturing at the Examination Schools, J.R.R.T. had reached retirement age. He gave his farewell speech in a Valedictory Lecture at the University in that year and emphasised in that speech his lifelong belief in the good of learning and of 'all fields of study and enquiry . . . Their roots are in the desire for knowledge, and their life is maintained by those who pursue some love or curiosity for its own sake, without reference even to personal improvement.' Ronald gave up his room in College and found that he had to fit a large part of his library into the house. Eventually the problem was solved by turning the garage (Ronald and Edith had not owned a car since the early 1940s) into a combined office and study. During the 1960s his international fame grew to such an extent that he was no longer able to cope with his correspondence single-handed and had to employ a part-time secretary, who would work with him in the converted garage. Over the years some became good friends, among them, Phyllis Jenkinson, Naomi Collyer and Elisabeth Lumsden, to whom Ronald and Edith were grateful for help and kindness far exceeding their official duties.

J.R.R.T. and Edith celebrating their
Golden Wedding Anniversary

The most exciting family event during this time was our parents' Golden Wedding in 1966, celebrated over several days in great contrast to the modesty of their Silver Wedding! A big gathering was held at Merton College at which Donald Swann performed his song cycle *The Road Goes Ever On* based on J.R.R.T.'s poems from *The Hobbit* and *The Lord of the Rings*. There was also a splendid lunch party. Cards, telegrams and gifts flooded in, including a beautiful bouquet of fifty golden roses sent from Sir Stanley Unwin.

Rayner Unwin had succeeded his father, Sir Stanley, as head of George Allen & Unwin Publishers, although he had been involved in Tolkien affairs since writing a report for his father on *The Hobbit* at the age of ten, receiving a shilling for his efforts. He continued to play an enormously important part in all the stages of J.R.R.T.'s progress towards becoming an internationally famous author, and J.R.R.T. held him in very high regard.

ABOVE: *Edith, 1965*

RIGHT: *Lawyer Dick Williamson and publisher Rayner Unwin with J.R.R.T., 1968*

Sadly, after this period, Edith's health deteriorated due to arthritis, which made walking increasingly difficult and climbing stairs almost impossible. Our parents took regular holidays in Bournemouth, staying at the comfortable, but not too grand, Hotel Miramar. They both loved the sea and the warmer, drier climate eased Edith's pain. With plenty of time and the financial freedom born of literary success they began to visit Bournemouth more and more frequently. They invited the family and old friends to visit them at the Hotel Miramar, and made new friends, including the hotel's proprietors, Douglas and Minna Steele.

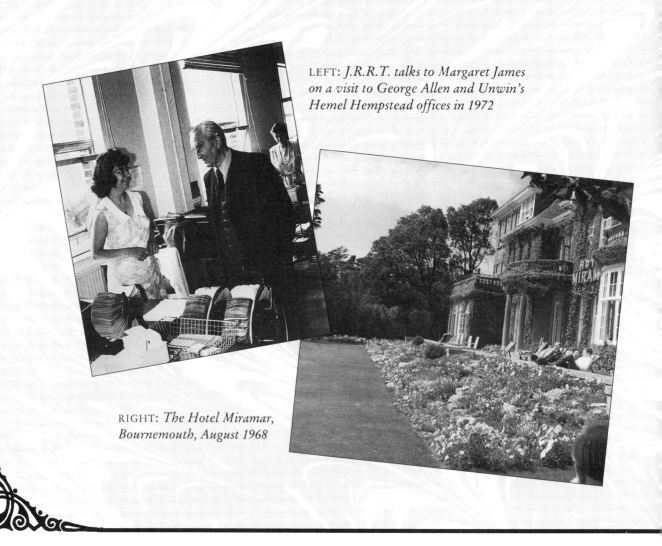

LEFT: *J.R.R.T. talks to Margaret James on a visit to George Allen and Unwin's Hemel Hempstead offices in 1972*

RIGHT: *The Hotel Miramar, Bournemouth, August 1968*

19 Lakeside Road

One morning Priscilla was astonished to receive a phone call from Edith saying that they had bought a bungalow in Bournemouth which they had seen only once, the day before! Just before leaving Sandfield Road, Ronald fell down the stairs, was taken to hospital and had to have surgery. With John's help and much practical assistance from Phyllis Jenkinson they eventually moved down to number 19 Lakeside Road, Bournemouth in August 1968. Here they lived in greater luxury than they had ever known, for despite the wealth generated by Ronald's writing, they both retained a great simplicity in the way they lived. Now, for the first time they enjoyed the comforts of central heating and a bathroom each; while Edith was as excited as a young bride at the sophistication of their new kitchen! Again, the garage was converted into a study and

Edith, John, Ronald and Michael, April 1969

Joy Hill with J.R.R.T.

office where Joy Hill, who worked for Allen & Unwin, would often come to help him with his correspondence, as his popularity spread and letters poured in from fans all over the world, but especially reflecting his extraordinary cult status in the USA. (So did phone calls: J.R.R.T. was incensed to answer the phone in the middle of the night to hear an American lady ask, 'Is that you, Professor? I just wanted to say "hello"!' To which he very angrily replied, 'I just want to say "goodbye"!' and replaced the receiver with considerable alacrity.) Joy became a devoted friend to our parents and paid many visits to Bournemouth, combining work with pleasure.

It was during this period that the Tolkien Society was founded by Vera Chapman, who, now in her nineties, still continues to be very much involved in the Society. Different groups meet regularly all over Britain, and publish magazines, and each September hold an Oxonmoot - a commemorative weekend in Oxford. There are now Tolkien Societies all over the world, from America to Borneo! J.R.R.T. was delighted to receive a portfolio of drawings from Margarethe, later to become Queen of Denmark: of the many hundreds of illustrations of his work sent to him, these were among the few that he admired, and they were later published in a special edition of *The Lord of the Rings* by the Folio Society.

Vera Chapman

However, Ronald found the break from Oxford after so many years very hard to bear. He felt cut off from the academic world, and from his family: for the first time none of us lived close to them. But, in compensation, he could see that Edith was happy, despite her growing infirmity. A shy person except with those she knew well, she developed in her old age a kind of self-confidence, partly based on Ronald's success and prosperity, but to a great extent on her own inner strengths of character, and during this time she made many friends.

After a mercifully short illness Edith died in a Bournemouth nursing home in November 1971 at the age of eighty-two. Ronald decided to return to Oxford, and Merton College offered him a flat at 21 Merton Street, which proved to be a happy solution for him in his great bereavement. Here he could be private without being too isolated.

In the last eighteen months of his life he continued to be very active, seeing family and friends, enjoying the proximity of college life, and being the recipient of further honours: the CBE, and an Honorary Doctorate of Letters from Oxford, both in 1972.

J.R.R.T. waiting to receive his D.Litt. with the Vice Chancellor, Sir Alan Bullock

The inevitable loneliness of life without Edith and the sadness of giving up his own home was tempered by the kindness of Charlie and Mavis Carr, who worked on the domestic staff of Merton College. They became devoted to J.R.R.T. and, in addition to looking after his flat, would invite him to meals with their family. His simplicity and especial love of children made him a particular favourite with their two young grand-daughters.

In July 1973 he travelled up to Edinburgh with Priscilla to receive his last public honour. Here they stayed with his old friend, Angus Macintosh, once his pupil and now Professor of English, and his wife Barbara. He thoroughly enjoyed the several days of festivities with apparently little sign of strain or tiredness. But this was to be almost his last public appearance: less than two months later he died.

21 Merton Street

His final journey was to return to Bournemouth in late August 1973, to stay with friends. He was taken seriously ill and died a few days later, on 2 September, in Bournemouth less than two years after Edith's death.

The funeral took place in Oxford at the Church of St Anthony of Padua in Headington, which he had attended for many years, with John the chief celebrant at the Mass. He was buried beside Edith in Wolvercote Cemetery. The gravestone reads 'Edith Mary Tolkien, Lúthien, 1889-1971. John Ronald Reuel Tolkien, Beren, 1892-1973', in reference to J.R.R.T.'s story of the love between Beren, a mortal man, and Lúthien, an elf maiden in *The Silmarillion*.

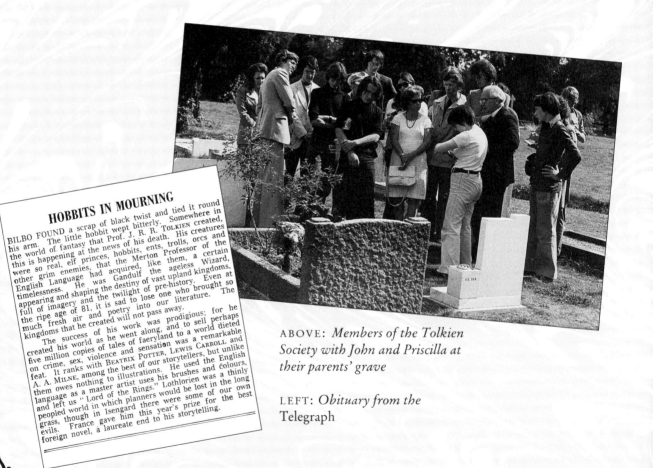

HOBBITS IN MOURNING

BILBO FOUND a scrap of black twist and tied it round his arm. The little hobbit wept bitterly. Somewhere in the world of fantasy that Prof. J. R. R. TOLKIEN created, this is happening at the news of his death. His creatures were so real, elf princes, hobbits, ents, trolls, orcs and other grim enemies, that the Merton Professor of the English Language had acquired, like them, a certain timelessness. He was Gandulf the ageless Wizard, appearing and shaping the destiny of vast upland kingdoms, full of imagery and the twilight of pre-history. Even at the ripe age of 81, it is sad to lose one who brought so much fresh air and poetry into our literature. The kingdoms that he created will not pass away.

The success of his work was prodigious; for he created his world as he went along, and to sell perhaps five million copies of tales of faeryland to a world dieted on crime, sex, violence and sensation was a remarkable feat. It ranks with BEATRIX POTTER, LEWIS CARROLL and A. A. MILNE, among the best of our storytellers, but unlike them owes nothing to illustrations. He used the English language as a master artist uses his brushes and colours, and left us "Lord of the Rings." Lothlorien was a thinly peopled world in which planners would be lost in the long grass, though in Isengard there were some of our own evils. France gave him this year's prize for the best foreign novel, a laureate end to his storytelling.

ABOVE: *Members of the Tolkien Society with John and Priscilla at their parents' grave*

LEFT: *Obituary from the Telegraph*

So **'Hobbist**, an advocate or adherent of Hobbism, a disciple of Hobbes; *attrib.* = HOBBESIAN. **Ho'bbistical** *a.*, of, pertaining to, or according to the Hobbists. **'Hobbize** *v. intr.*, to philosophize in the way of Hobbes.

1681 BAXTER *Search Schism* ii. 19 Swearers and Atheists, *Hobbists and wicked men are members of their Church. **1756-82** J. WARTON *Ess. Pope* (1806) II. 47 With all the malignity of a discontented Hobbist. **1857** BUCKLE *Civiliz.* I. vii. 357 Every man who ventured to think for himself was stigmatized as a Hobbist, or as it was sometimes called a Hobbian. **1874** GREEN *Short Hist.* ix. § 1. 602 The Hobbist philosophy. **1754** EDWARDS *Freed. Will* IV. vii. 238 He only acts by an *Hobbistical Fatality. **1696** J. EDWARDS *Demonstr. Exist. God* II. 109 We must not surmise that this great man began to *Hobbize.

hobbit ('hɒbɪt). [See below.] In the tales of J. R. R. Tolkein (1892-1973): one of an imaginary people, a small variety of the human race, that gave themselves this name (meaning 'hole-dweller') but were called by others *halflings*, since they were half the height of normal men. Also *attrib.* and *Comb.* Hence **'hobbitish** *a.*, resembling a hobbit, hobbit-like; **'hobbitomane**, a devotee of hobbits; **'hobbitry**, the cult of hobbits; hobbits collectively, or their qualities.

1937 J. R. R. TOLKEIN *Hobbit* i. 11 In a hole in the ground there lived a hobbit. **1947** C. S. LEWIS in *Ess. presented to C. Williams* 104 The Hobbit escapes the danger of degenerating into mere plot and excitement by a very curious shift of tone. As the humour and homeliness of the early chapters, the sheer 'Hobbitry', dies away we pass insensibly into the world of epic. **1954** J. R. R. TOLKIEN *Fellowship of Ring* 7 The memoirs of the renowned Hobbits, Bilbo and Frodo. *Ibid.* 11 A few notes..are here collected from Hobbit-lore. *Ibid.* 20 The Thain was..captain of the Shire-muster and the Hobbitry-in-arms. *Ibid.* 46 It was a tendency of hobbit-holes to get cluttered up. **1955** —— *Return of King* 416 *Hobbit* is an invention. In the Westron the word used, when this people was referred to at all, was *banakil* 'halfling'. But ..the folk of the Shire and of Bree used the word *kuduk*... It seems likely that *kaduk* was a worn-down form of *kûd-dûkan* [= 'hole-dweller']. The latter I have translated..by *holbytla* ['hole-builder']; and *hobbit* provides a word that might well be a worn-down form of *holbytla*, if the name had occurred in our own ancient language. **1962** *Listener* 22 Nov. 881/3 The more ambitious hobbit saga, *The Lord of the Rings*. *Ibid.*, To those who are already hobbitomanes, this book is bound to be a delight. **1966** *New Statesman* 11 Nov. 701/2 The newest and richest site of hobbitry is the American campus, where students are said to greet each other with hobbitish salutations such as 'May your beard never grow less'. **1968** *Listener* 20 June 790/3 Professer Tolkien was thinking of the average, ambling Englishman when he wrote about his hobbits. **1970** H. PERRY *Human Be-In* i. 20 The consistently good people in the Tolkien books are Hobbits and they have the lowliest status of all the groups of characters in the books. The hippies thought of themselves as being or becoming Hobbits; from time to time as the winter wore on, a sign would appear in the window of one of their gathering places to this effect: Do not add to the street confusion this weekend... Be good little Hobbits and stay home.

Time continues to draw on towards the end of the twentieth century, and sadly only three now of J.R.R. Tolkien's four children can celebrate the centenary of his birth, Michael having died of leukaemia in 1984. Our father may have died in 1973 but, one hundred years from his birth, his literary fame lives on, and we hope that his work will continue to give pleasure and inspiration to succeeding generations of readers.

The Laughing Philosopher